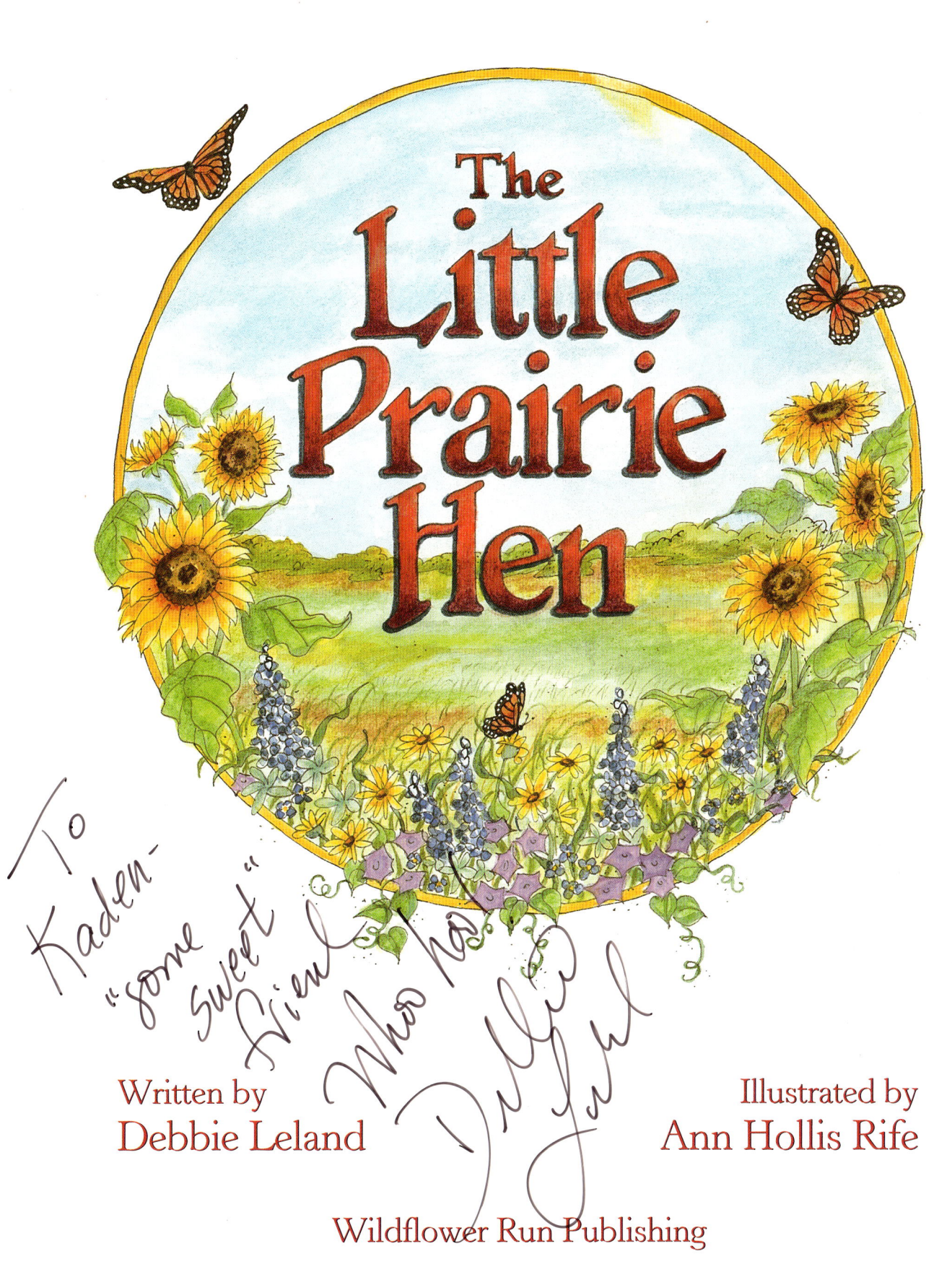

The Little Prairie Hen

Written by
Debbie Leland

Illustrated by
Ann Hollis Rife

Wildflower Run Publishing

The Coastal County Fair and Rodeo was finally here. The prairie dog, the buffalo, and the horned toad were as excited as bucking broncos busting out of their gates.

"Hmmmph," said the little prairie hen. "A waste of perfectly good time if you ask..." But before she finished, a pecan fell to the ground.

"Howdee!" she shouted. "Now, I can make my pecan pie."

"Sounds as good as a horseback ride in the countryside," said the prairie dog.

"Good as a ticket to the tractor pull," said the buffalo.

The horned toad spat. "Pttt, pttt, pttt."

"Who will help me gather the pecans?" asked the little prairie hen.

"Oh, I wish I could, Honey," said the prairie dog fluffing her hair, "but I'm fixin' to do my do. I'm gonna be the Coastal County Queen, you know."

"Now Darlin', I want to help," said the buffalo. "You know I do. But every rodeo has to have a clown. And I want to be the best clown ever."

The horned toad sat and spat. "Pttt, pttt, pttt."

"Y'all are *some* friends," she said in a tiff. "I'll just gather the pecans myself."

She collected pecans one by one until her burlap bag was as heavy as a handful of horseshoes.

"Now, who will help me shell the pecans?" asked the little prairie hen.

"I wish I could, Honey," said the prairie dog lining her lips, "but I might break a nail."

The buffalo galloped around and around on his stick horse.

The horned toad sat and spat. "Pttt, pttt, pttt."

"Y'all are *some* friends," said the little prairie hen in a tiff. "I'll just shell the pecans myself." So she shelled and shelled until her feathers ached.

"Who will help me make the pie?" asked the little prairie hen.

"I wish I could, Honey, but I've got my queenly duties," said the prairie dog parading past the prickly pear cacti, the golden wing dragonflies, and the mockingbirds by the fence posts.

"Later gator," said the buffalo. He ran and jumped into a barrel. The barrel fell over and rolled down the hill faster than a roadrunner racing a jackrabbit.

"Ay yi yi," he cried.

The horned toad sat and spat. "Pttt, pttt, pttt."

"Y'all are *some* friends," said the little prairie hen in a tiff. "I'll just make the pie myself." She rolled the dough and crimped the edges with a fork. She filled the pie shell, and placed the pecans on top.

By the time she put the pie in the oven, the little prairie hen had worked up a sweat. She wiped her brow with her bandana, poured herself a glass of iced tea, and plopped down into her chair.

"Whew," she said. "That was hard work."

When the little prairie hen took the pie out of the oven, the sweet, fresh-baked aroma floated out the window and covered Coastal County like bluebonnets and bees; like monarchs on milkweed; like sunflowers in summertime.

Just as she put the pie on the table, the prairie dog, the buffalo, and the horned toad burst into the room. The little prairie hen was not surprised. She knew her pie could make 'possums drool and coyotes howl.

"I wonder," she said. "Who will help me eat my pie?"

"Oh Honey," said the prairie dog, "I've got to squeeze into my bathing suit."

"Not I," said the buffalo.

The horned toad shook his head.

"I guess I'll just eat the pie myself," said the little prairie hen.

"Why don't you come with us?" asked the buffalo. "It'll be more fun than a hayride in the moonlight."

She looked at her pie. She looked at her friends.

"Oh, I might as well go," she said. The three friends winked at each other and smiled.

As soon as the little prairie hen saw the roller coaster, she was glad she'd come. She rode the Ferris wheel with the buffalo, shared cotton candy with the horned toad, and played carnival games with the prairie dog.

She even won a goldfish named Fred. "This fair is *some* fun," said the little prairie hen.

She had forgotten all about her pecan pie.

At the beauty contest, the little prairie hen cheered when the prairie dog twirled her baton like a Broadway star. "Howdee!" cried the little prairie hen. "That's my friend, the Coastal County Queen."

The little prairie hen held her breath when a bull named "Texas Tornado" snorted and stomped his feet at a cowboy he'd thrown.

"Oh no," she cried as the buffalo tiptoed up to Texas T. and pulled his tail.

That bull, steam coming out of his nostrils like an old-time train, turned and charged. The buffalo jumped inside a barrel.

Kaboom!

Horns hit the barrel like lightning splitting an old oak tree.

Texas T. pushed the buffalo around the arena like a tumbleweed blowing through town.

"Ay yi yi," cried the buffalo as the cowboy climbed to safety.

"Whoo hoo!" hollered the little prairie hen. "That's my friend, the bravest rodeo clown in the arena."

At the watermelon-seed-spitting contest, the armadillo was in the lead.

"Go H.T.," cheered the little prairie hen.

The horned toad puffed his cheeks like he was filling a hot-air balloon, and he spat. "Pttttttttttttttttt!"

His seed flew like a rocket ship shooting into space, forty-five feet and three inches, a new Coastal County record.

The little prairie hen clapped and clapped. "That's my friend," she cried. "The seed-spitting champ."

"Come on y'all," said the prairie dog. "Follow me."

They arrived at the Baking Tent just in time to hear the judge announce, "And the winning entry for the Best Recipe Contest is Miss Little Prairie Hen for her pecan pie." The judge handed her the biggest blue ribbon she'd ever seen.

"Why, I never," said the little prairie hen beaming. "Y'all are *some* friends."

When the pictures for the newspaper had all been taken, the prairie dog said hungrily, "*Now*, I will help you eat your pie."

"Hmmmph," said the little prairie hen. "I gathered the pecans myself. I shelled the pecans myself. I made the pie myself. I worked my feathers to the spine, all by myself."

"Pretty pleassse," said the buffalo. "With ice cream and dewberries on top."

She looked at her pie. She looked at her friends.

"Well," she said. "Who will help me clean up the mess?"

"Oh, I will," said the prairie dog.

"I will," said the buffalo.

"Me pttttoo," spat the horned toad.

So the four friends shared the best blue ribbon pecan pie in all of Coastal County. As soon as they finished, the little prairie hen kicked off her boots, fluffed out her feathers, and relaxed on the porch swing all by herself.

"Why bless their hearts," said the little prairie hen. "I have *some sweet* friends."

The Attwater's Prairie-Chicken

The Attwater's prairie-chicken is *some* bird!

The Plains Indians modeled their dances after the prairie-chicken's courtship ritual. The male birds perform on a booming ground, or lek. This is a flat area of short grass on the prairie. They inflate their tympani, the orange sacs on the sides of their necks. They erect their tail feathers, and the long feathers behind their head called pinnae. They bow and boom to get the female's attention. Booming is the low sound the male bird makes.

Ooo-loo-woo! They send the sound across the prairie. The sound, similar to blowing across the top of a glass soda bottle, can be heard up to one-half mile away. They stomp their feet in a frenzy. They cackle at each other. They charge at each other. They jump. They stomp and boom some more. Their feet move so fast that you can hardly see them. They challenge each other. Feathers fly. Prairie-chickens fly.

The females will choose the strongest male, the one holding the middle of the booming ground, for breeding. So every morning from February through April the coastal prairie, with its bunch grasses, little bluestem, Indiangrass, and switchgrass, comes to life with the prairie-chicken's dazzling display.

It is *some* show, or it used to be.

The Attwater's prairie-chicken (Tympanuchus cupido attwateri) is now one of the most endangered birds in the world. Named after Henry Philemon Attwater (1854-1931), an English naturalist, the bird is seventeen inches long, eats green leaves, seeds and insects, and has an average life span of two to three years in the wild. A member of the grouse family, it is related to the Greater prairie-chicken and the now-extinct Heath hen.

There used be more than a million Attwater's prairie-chickens living on six million acres of coastal prairie across Louisiana and Texas. But because of urban and industrial growth, and over-grazing, most of the coastal prairie is gone. There are fewer than fifty Attwater's prairie-chickens living in the wild today.

Wild Attwater's prairie-chickens are only found in two places, both in Texas. One is the Attwater Prairie Chicken National Wildlife Refuge established in 1972, near Eagle Lake. The other is the Texas City Prairie Preserve owned by The Nature Conservancy.

A captive breeding program and habitat management are some of the steps being taken to save the endangered bird. There is even an Adopt-a-Prairie-Chicken program for those individuals or groups who want to help. More information about adopting a prairie-chicken can be found at www.tpwd.state.tx.us/apc or by calling (512) 389-4644.

As the Plains Indians noticed many years ago, the Attwater's prairie-chicken is a special bird. By working together to restore the coastal prairie habitat, perhaps the Attwater's prairie-chicken's spectacular show might go on and on for many years to come. All the Attwater's prairie-chickens need is a little help from their friends.

In memory of my grandmother, Marjorie Aschwanden, who gave me
so many wonderful memories. – D.L.

To my mother and father, Laura Henderson and Burtis Hollis, who never told me
"Not I" when I needed their support, encouragement, and love. – A.H.R.

First Edition, 2003
Text copyright © 2003 by Debbie Leland
Illustrations copyright © 2003 by Ann Hollis Rife

All rights reserved. No part of this publication may be reproduced or transmitted in any form
or by any means, electronic or mechanical, including photocopy, recording, or any information
storage and retrieval system, without permission in writing from the publisher.

Pre-press by David O. Cooper
Printed in China through Morris Press, Ltd.
10 9 8 7 6 5 4 3

Library of Congress Control Number: 2002117698

Leland, Debbie, The little prairie hen/Debbie Leland: illustrated by Ann Hollis Rife

p. cm.

Summary: The little prairie hen bakes a pecan pie in this Southern version of *The Little Red Hen*.
Her friends, the prairie dog, the buffalo, and the horned toad surprise her in the end.
[1. Hens – Juvenile Fiction   2. Animals – Juvenile Fiction   3. Texas-Juvenile Fiction
4. Fairy Tale   5. Attwater's Prairie Chicken – Juvenile Fiction]
I. Rife, Ann Hollis, ill.   II. Title.
[E]
ISBN 0-9667086-3-6
ISBN 978-0-9667086-3-9

Little Prairie Hen's Pecan Pie

2 eggs beaten
1 cup dark corn syrup
1/2 cup sugar
1 Tbsp. flour
1 Tbsp. melted butter
1 tsp. vanilla
2 cups pecans
1 9" unbaked pie shell

Preheat oven to 375 degrees.
Mix ingredients.
Add 1 1/2 cup pecans. Pour into pie shell.
Arrange 1/2 cup pecans on top of pie
(cover with mix)
Turn oven to 300 degrees.
Bake 45-50 minutes or until toothpick comes out clean.

Wildflower Run Publishing
P.O. Box 9656
College Station, TX 77842
www.aggiegoose.com